Foreword by Kiese Laymon

MAMA'S
BOOK *of*
Prayers

PRAYER, PROMPTS, POWER & PRAISE

Workbook

DR. CAROLYN COLEMAN
AND CATHERINE COLEMAN-SMITH

Jai Publishing House Incorporated
1230 Peachtree Street NE, 19th Floor
Atlanta, Georgia 30309
www.jaipublishing.com

Book Cover Design by Jai Publishing House Incorporated

Design and Layout by Davor Nikolic

Illustration designed by pikisuperstar; Harryarts; Freepik.com; rawpixel.com; orchidart / Freepik

Ordering Information: Quantity sales. Special discounts are available on quantity purchases by corporations, associations, and others. For details, contact the publisher at the address above.

Printed in the United States of America

ISBN:978-1-7342352-1-0

This Workbook belongs to:

_____

(insert picture)

Contents

Foreword

By Kiese Laymon

My grandmother, Catherine Coleman, taught my auntie, Bishop Carolyn Coleman to pray years be-fore she taught me. Though all students should be equally valued, some students value the lessons of their teachers more than others. In our family, though we were all diligent students, my auntie has used the lessons we were taught by my grandmother most profoundly.

Where many of us purport or pretend to live God-fearing lives or God-loving lives, my auntie Bishop Carolyn Coleman always believed in creating lives where God was honored.

This wholly original book of prayers is more than a how-to book; it is a magnificent aid, a blessed offering pleading with all of us to hone our practice of loving God through the daily honoring of the abundance God has made possible. This book, like my auntie, is wise in its ability to look in backwards and innovative in its desire to wander forward. I Love my auntie and I'm thankful for her eternal love of us. She is teaching all of us how to tenderly honor God.

Introduction

I was born for purpose. Raised for success. Washed from the fear of failure. I am transformed and blessed through the power of prayer.

——————— Dr. Carolyn Coleman ———————

This book, like my life, is born out of a love of God, family, friends, colleagues, foes, and hidden and revealed enemies. Every circumstance brought me closer to God through the *Power of Prayer*.

There are prayers of proclamation of faith, prayers of supplication, and prayers for request. The good news is that scripture reminds us that not only does the Father hear our prayers, but He is Sovereign and honors faithfulness. Isn't it good to know that although we are not perfect, He is pleased by our commitment to trusting His "Word"?

The goal of **PRAYER, PROMPTS, POWER & PRAISE** is to enhance your prayer life and improve your ability to understand how scripture is the tool for personally communicating His Word. The workbook is the application of your prayer life through writing out your prayer strategy. You will see the Word come to life right before your eyes!

Let's start with writing out our first prayer strategy! Use the Bible you are most comfortable with learning and understanding the Word of God, and write them below in the respective boxes.

JEREMIAH 1:11-12

We recognize the need to pray in and out of season and the need to petition on behalf of others.

JAMES 5:14-16

2 Corinthians 12: 9-10

We pray because we simply delight in communicating and worshipping Him.

Psalms 95:6-7

We pray because the thoughts of our heart bring us into the presence of God.

Psalms **33:11**

We pray because the God in us demands that we ask, seek and search for divine wisdom in order to receive the downloads of His Visions for us.

Genesis **13:14-18**

PRAYER, PROMPTS, POWER AND PRAISE is a collection of life lessons and affirmations that have molded my character and shaped my divine purpose. This collection of prayers was written to inspire, assist, empower and help one develop a strong (or stronger) prayer life that will set the tra-jectory of your life and all that you touch.

For every daughter and son of the faith, every family member, student, church family, friend and foe that have called on me to pray, this book is for you.

Life taught me to love the unlovable and forgive the unforgivable because it set me free. I pray that the prayers, the prompts, and the praises will elevate your mind and open the windows and doors of your heart so you can walk in oneness with the Creator.

This book is an offering of love that I pray will heal, deliver, and set you and those you love free.

Free you from shame and disappointments.

Free you from doubt and fear and cause you to be transformed and elevated into greatness.

Read and share the prayers and complete the prompts, and watch the praise arise and the Power of God ignite and take full control. Your greatness is never defined by what is outward but by the in-ward thoughts, actions, and deeds.

Morning Meditation
Daily Prayers

Psalm 19:14

Daily Our Father Prayer

SCRIPTURE: _____

Our Father, which art in heaven, I ask for divine revelations and manifestations. I petition Your throne humbly, asking for the Holy Spirit to guide me into all truth that I may walk in the path of righteousness. I am open and available to receive spiritual enlightenment that can only come from you.

_____

_____

_____

_____

_____

_____

_____

_____

Daily Prayer of Salvation

SCRIPTURE:

You are my light and salvation. May Your spiritual gifts be added unto me with wisdom, knowledge and understanding. I will always point to the cross and be grateful for Your life, death, and resurrection. Thank You for loving, saving, and dying for me. AMEN

Daily Prayer for Mercy

SCRIPTURE: _____

Lord, I thank You for being my friend and a keeper of my soul. Please continue to extend Your hand of love, mercy, grace and favor in my direction. Let me live in peace with my fellow man. May my heart never forget to forgive. I ask for a forgiving spirit that I may be forgiven. May Your love and mercy be the compass that guides me daily. I am graced in favor. Wealth and riches be-long to me because You are my God. Thank You for everlasting love and favor. I lift Your name up high. I rise early to tell You that I love You and thank You for the seen and unseen blessings that You have sent my way. Let me daily operate with a Spirit of truth, love, integrity, happiness, peace, abundance, and joy. In Jesus' Name I pray. AMEN

Daily Prayer of Protection & Covering

SCRIPTURE:

Dear God, please dress me in the whole armor of God, so that I may be able to stand against the schemes of the devil. Please cancel every trick and plan of the devil. Make me a discerner of Your truth and Your divine revelations. AMEN

Put on the whole armour of God, that ye may be able to stand against the wiles of the devil.

-EPHESIANS **6:11**

Daily Our Father Prayer

SCRIPTURE: _____

Holy Father teach me how to give my life to You. I need help in dying to my flesh. Please give me divine revelation to live, forgive and trust. I need Your help in these areas of my life daily. AMEN

_____

_____

_____

_____

_____

_____

_____

_____

_____

_____

Let Your Word Live in Me

I find myself

(feel free to replace with your own words)

- _____ Sleeping In Wrong Beds
- _____ Walking In Unforgiveness
- _____ Constantly Comparing Myself to Others
- _____ Judging Others
- _____ Feeling Like I Am Not Good Enough
- _____ Blaming Others For My Wrongs
- _____ Fighting
- _____ Cursing
- _____ Being Vindictive
- _____ Being Rebellious
- _____ Hating My Life
- _____ Angry
- _____ Being Mean
- _____ Wanting To Give Up
- _____ Being Afraid
- _____ Being Paranoid
- _____ Being Depressed
- _____ Hating My Body
- _____ Being the Victim
- _____ Lying To Myself
- _____ Over Thinking Everything
- _____ Rehearsing The Past
- _____ fill in the blank
- _____ fill in the blank
- _____ fill in the blank
- _____ fill in the blank

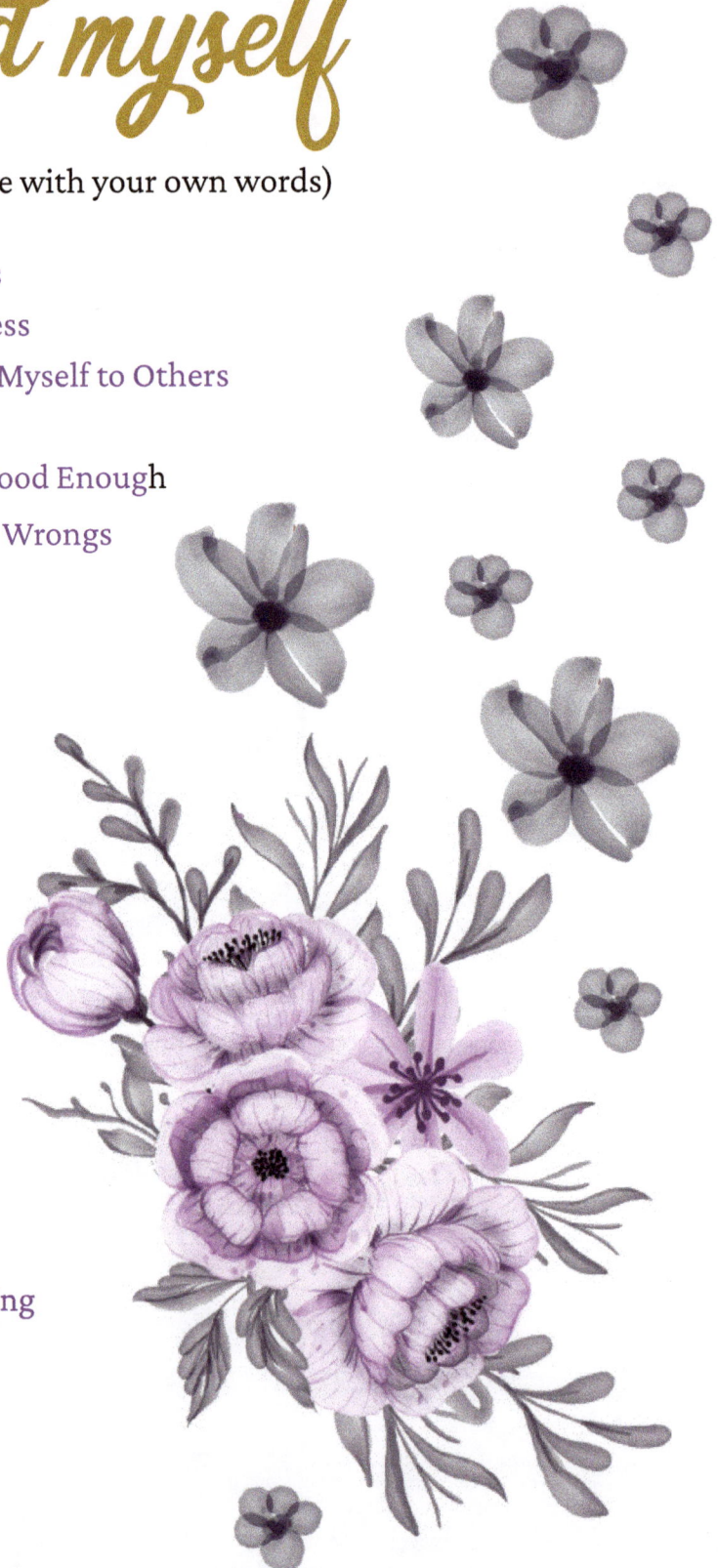

Self-deliverance starts with confessing your sins,
weaknesses, struggles, challenges, yokes of bondage...
and applying the Balm of God's Word to it.

This will require a little of studying and research:
Find a scripture for every topic or challenge you wrote
in the previous section.

| Word / Topic | Scripture / Prayer Strategy |

| Word / Topic | Scripture / Prayer Strategy |

| Word / Topic | Scripture / Prayer Strategy |

Prayer of Forgiveness of Sin

Dear Heavenly Father,

Thank You for Your unfailing love and compassion toward me. Thank You for being a present help in times of joy, sorrow, doubt, and guilt. My heart is grieved because of wrong choices I have made. My desires to rebel against You have brought me to my knees. Forgive me once again and teach me how to live for You. I turn from sin, forsaking my evil ways. Please forgive me for caus-ing harm to myself, others, especially those who have toiled and loved me unconditionally. Forgive me for directly or indirectly causing harm to:

_____

_____

_____

_____

_____

_____

_____

Help Me Forgive Myself For...

Help Me To Forgive My Family For...

Help Me To Forgive Others For...

Help Me Press Forward Forgiving
& Forget-ting the Past...

Create In Me a Clean Heart

Psalm 51:10

I ask that you restore my mind, spirit, and soul.

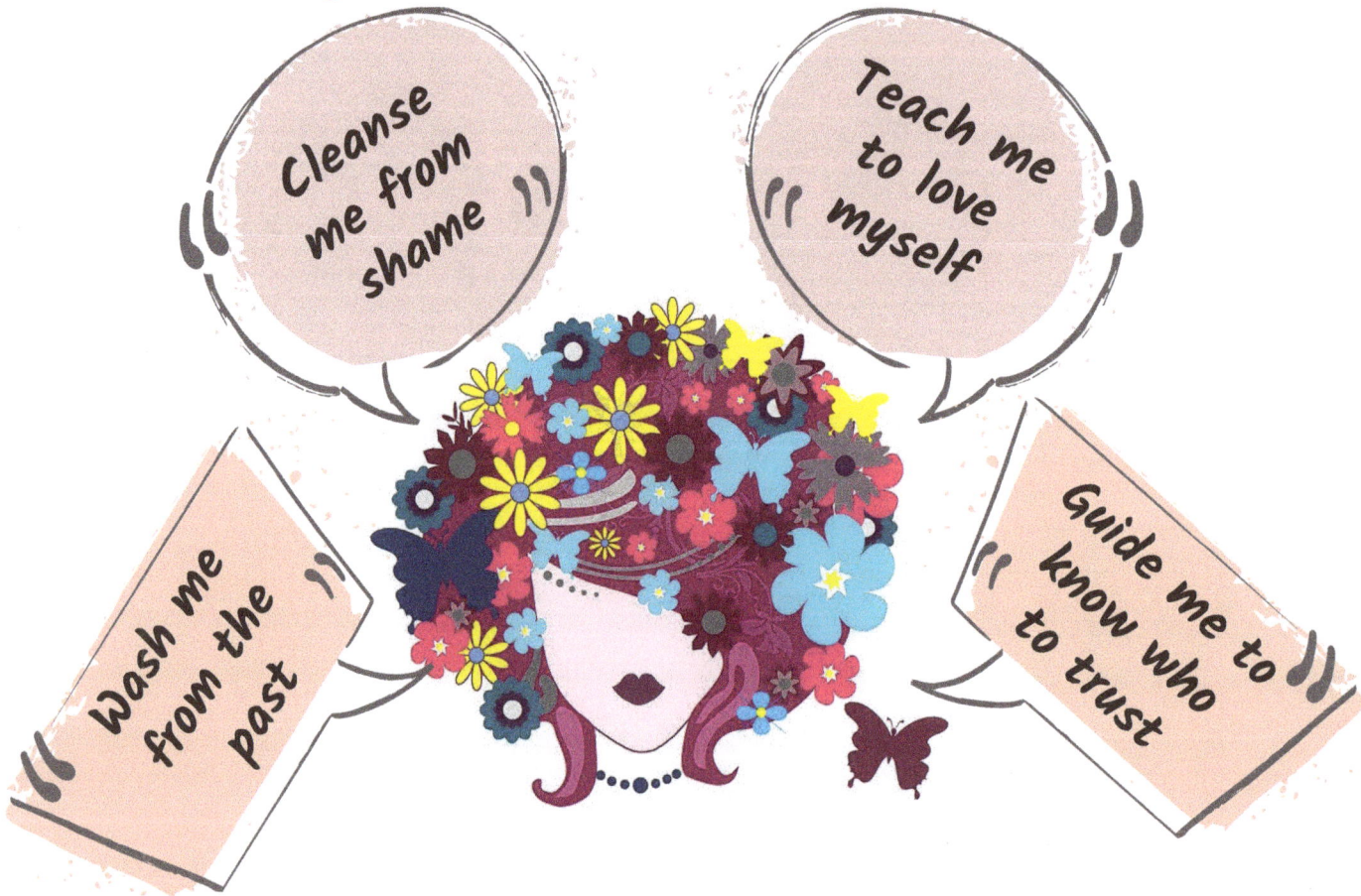

"Cleanse me from shame"

"Teach me to love myself"

"Wash me from the past"

"Guide me to know who to trust"

What areas do you need God's help? Give them to the Father in prayer, by releasing them on to paper (and out of your heart and mind).

Post clipped out images or words from magazines, newspa-pers, or draw your own of what your life would look like FREE from those things you wrote in the box on the previ-ous page.

I Need Your Help!

I need Your help and strength to keep my heart and mind stayed on the things that are for my great-est good and prosperous to my soul. I need and want a discerning spirit. I ask You this day to bless me with a discerning spirit and a heart and mind that will desire You and bless me with a spirit of truth.

I ask You to usher me into a mindset of victory over every thought that would beset me and sepa-rate me from my promise and Your love. I surrender my will to You. Please give me a Christ-like mind.

Thanks for hearing my honest prayer. I press forward to the greater and seek Your face for wis-dom, knowledge and understanding. AMEN

_____

_____

_____

_____

_____

_____

_____

Prayer For a Sound Mind

I ask you to help me with my emotional triggers that lead to bad decisions and wrong choices. AMEN

List several bad choices or bad decisions:

Identify your emotional triggers:

What makes you tick? What sets you off? What rubs you the wrong way?

How do you respond?

How do you feel "after" you respond?

How do you move on, because it is important that you do?

Write your prayer here.

Petition for Help in Time of Trouble

Help me, Loving God, and flood my heart with peace. I know that you can deliver and provide consolation.

YES, I FEEL... (Please select a word from below that ap-plies)

.... Lost

.... Confused

.... Uncertain of my purpose

.... Conflicted in the choices I have made

.... Misdirected

.... Angry

.... Rejected

.... Not Good Enough

.... Unworthy

.... write your own word

.... write your own word

.... write your own word

Reveal me to me. Open my eyes to the truth that has been hidden from me. Let me walk in the truth of Your Word. You gave me the gift of peace. Today, I receive it with love.

_____

_____

_____

_____

_____

_____

_____

_____

_____

_____

I Am Enough in Jesus Name

Affirmation

I am complete and made whole through the love of Jesus Christ

NOTES

Transform My Mind

I need direction and I trust that You know what is best for me. I need courage to face my today and believe for a better tomorrow. I pray that You would grant whatever is best for my greater good. I seek Your plan for my life that I may fulfill my destiny. Help me to overcome my doubts and fears and walk in power.

Resurrect me from the scars of childhood and the abuses of adulthood. Let the plans and purposes You have for me be revealed in Jesus' Name. AMEN

Lord I need you to help to

(Fill In The Blank):

_____

_____

_____

_____

_____

_____

_____

Prayers of Thanksgiving for Your Children

Father God, I thank You for my child(ren).

LIST THEIR FULL NAMES HERE
(be creative and include pictures or something reminding you of that)

The Character of God

"No," is not rejection. It is just someone's opinion

Never quit on their dream

Visions to dream big and bigger

Belief and faith that moves mountains

To obey quickly and with accuracy

A trustworthy spirit

Determination and Drive

A spirit of excellence

Saturate with a spirit of endurance

Operate with a spirit of integrity

Make decision(s) free from emotion

Lord, instill in them...

Ability to comprehend

Understanding

Knowledge

Wisdom

A humble spirit

A heart that will love God

An obedient spirit

Prayer Prompts to Pray Over Your Children

Father God, thank You for keeping my {son/daughter} safe through the night. I ask You to order the footsteps of (NAME(S) of child(ren) and write a prayer for each child:

Thank You for showing them Your love and grace each day of their lives. Please supply my child(ren)'s every need according to Your will. Be their health and wealth. Add the increase of abundance and wisdom to maintain the blessings that only You can give.

Teach them how to be responsible, resourceful, and thankful for all things. Establish their thoughts and reveal divine revelations on how to receive and walk in increase and multiplication.

Your Word say that You give us the ability to obtain wealth. I ask You now to pour that ability over my child. Bless them to live the Abundant life in Christ according to your will. AMEN

DEUTERONOMY 8:18

A Mother's Prayer For Her Children

I ask You to cover them with Your Blood. I humbly ask You to shield them from harmful bullies, jealous spirits, angry and self- destructive spirits.

Build them up to walk in truth and love. Give them the strength and endurance to walk away from situations and environments that are harmful and detrimental to their destiny. Allow them to learn from their mistakes and quickly recover. I thank You for hearing and answering my prayer. AMEN

I ask you and thank You for traveling grace as they travel to and from school. I ask You to send Your protective angels to guard over them in the classroom, sporting events and any/ all extracur-ricular activities.

Minister to their teachers, administrators, and staff to teach and lead them with honor. I give You praise Almighty God, and thank You in advance for hearing and answering my prayer. AMEN

ISAIAH 65:24

A Prayer for Revelation

Father God I ask You to send a spirit of obedience and enlightenment to my (daughter's name(s)/son's name(s):

Parenting Prayer

Father God in me, show me how to be the parent that she/he needs. Teach me how to be a good mother and example for her/him to follow. Teach my child to be the change agent you would have her/him to be. Equip me to understand her/his needs and to identify her/his talents so that I may facilitate and aid in the cultivation of her/his gifts.

Provide the finances and networks so that your will is done. Position us to be ready when oppor-tunity comes. Teach us what to say and how to be diligent. Mold our hands that we may use them for your glory. Teach her/him discipline and how to honor your gifts. Bless my child with confi-dence in you. Never allow my child to be conceited or self-righteous. Speak through them so that their words will be prudent and just in your sight. I thank you for the gift of my child(ren). Today, I request for your will to be fulfilled and manifested in their lives. AMEN

Philippians 4:6

Affirmations To Teach Your Child

I AM Covered by the Blood of Jesus

I AM Fearfully and Wonderfully Made

I AM the Abundant Life in Christ

I AM Trustworthy and True

I AM Unstoppable

I AM Honest and Reliable

I AM Healthy, Wealthy and Wise

I AM Protected by I AM

I AM Loveable

I AM Very Bold and Very Courageous

I AM Living the Abundant Life in Christ

I AM Determined and
Committed to Succeed

Write your OWN affirmations.

Hint: It may be a good family time to create the affirmations togeth-er!

Daily Prayer For Children

Our Father which art in heaven. Hallowed be thy name, thy Kingdom come, thy will be done on earth as it is in heaven. Give us this day our daily bread and forgive us of our sins as we forgive our debtors. I petition Your will and seek Your counsel on behalf of:

Child's Name

Child's Name

Child's Name

Child's Name

Prayer for Provision

Heavenly Father,

Thank You for provision and for providing the needs for this day.
As You care for the birds, I know that

_____

_____

_____

_____

_____

_____

_____

_____

_____

_____

_____

YOU WILL TAKE CARE OF...

Please let the love of Jesus Christ be revealed in them today and
every day of their lives. I honor You this day and thank You for the comfort of
knowing that Your blessings are fresh and new every morning. AMEN

THIS IS MY PRAYER FOR TODAY...

I thank you for hearing and answering my prayers today. AMEN

Prayer for Knowledge and Understanding

Dear Lord,

I ask You to help my child(ren) to know right from wrong. Help my child/ren to listen and be atten-tive in school. Grant them the mindset to study and make good grades. Please instill a desire and a hunger to thirst and seek new knowledge daily. Increase their appetite for learning, comprehending, and applying knowledge to paper. Bless my child/ren with teachers who will inspire them and never bring harm.

Add qualities and characteristics specific to your child(ren)'s need(s):

Prayer for The Presence of God

Send your Holy Spirit so that they will make good choices and decisions. Please honor Your ser-vant's prayer, AMEN

Your Name

List your child(ren)'s name (s):

List your concerns for each of them:

Prayers of Protection for Children

Our Father, I cry out to You with worship and thanksgiving. Thank You for sending angels to watch over and protect my children from all hurt, harm and danger. Bind the hand of the enemy in Jesus' Name I pray. AMEN

Lord, in the Name of Your Son, Jesus Christ, I declare that no weapons formed against my child will prosper. That every force and spirit of wickedness is destroyed by the blood of Jesus shed at Calvary.

I go in agreement with Your word that my child is healed of all diseases, sickness, infirmities, and inflammations in the body. My child's mind is alert.

I bind all forms of witchcraft, sorcery, and unrighteous acts seen or sent; they will not penetrate the thoughts, dreams or ambitions of my child.

I call on the assigned angels from heaven to guard, guide, and protect my child. I call on You Al-mighty God to pour out blessings too numerous for them to receive. Armor and fight for them and with them, I pray. AMEN

Prayer for God to Bless Your Child Mind, Body and Soul

*T*ouch her/his mind, body, and soul. Thank You for the elevation and spiritual growth that will lead to joy, peace, love, happiness, and safety every day of her/his life. It is done in Jesus' Name. AMEN

Child's Name

_____

Child's Name

_____

Child's Name

_____

Child's Name

_____

God has not given my children a spirit of fear, but of power, love and a sound mind. Amen and Praise God.

2 Timothy 1:7

Prayer for Blood Covering

Dear God,

I ask You to keep and cover my child/ren daily. Cover them with the Blood of Jesus. Please keep them covered despite all their mishaps. You are Jehovah Nissi, the LORD who covers; You are our Eternal Banner. I thank You for your Faithfulness. AMEN

Prayer of Acknowledgment

I acknowledge that you are God. I freely accept your Precious Son, Jesus. I proclaim and receive him as LORD and Savior. I gratefully give you praise and acknowledge the Holy Spirit that is in operation in me. Your blessings are afresh and new every day. I thank you for your divine mercy and your loving grace extended to me daily. I accept Your gracious Gift, Jesus Christ, as My LORD and Savior.

GENESIS 17:1

ROMANS 6:16-18

Prayer of Confession

Write down your prayer of confessing your sins and accepting His forgiveness.

Romans 3:23-26

Pray that His will be done in your life and that His Holy Spirit will guide you. Ask that He will fill you with the fullness of all God has for you.

Prayer for Spiritual Understanding and Wisdom

Lord, I need to walk in wisdom, knowledge and understanding. Please help me now in Jesus' Name to be quick to listen, slow to speak and slow to anger. Usher in my heart a spirit of clarity of thought. Let Your anointing and faith navigate my every thought.

It is my desire to be a good steward over your word. Bless me to operate in a spirit of truth. AMEN

PROVERBS 2:6-8

PROVERBS 3:5

Prayer for Healing

Pray this prayer using these scriptures when you are sick, lonely, going through trials or interceding for others.

Lord, you are my healer. You are my strong tower. You are the source of my strength and the hope of my faith. Water me with your truth and fill me with your love. I trust the works of your mighty hand and align myself with your vision of my divine purpose. I thank you for divine healing even now. I shout over the mountains that are daily being removed from my life and the lives of my family. I thank you that your grace is sufficient for me. I love you and lift my hands in worship and praise for your mighty works. AMEN

JAMES 5:14-16

2 Corinthians 12:9-10

Prayer to Worship God

Lord, I will rise early in the morning to worship and give You praise. My lips will speak of Your many wondrous works. My heart will rejoice over the victories You have won on my behalf. My eyes cannot contain its water because of the love I feel flowing from You. I love You and thank You for all the blessings You have bestowed upon me and my family.

Psalm 95:6-7

Prayer for Protection from Evil

Holy Father, I ask You to protect my child(ren) from all evil. I ask You to let Your light be a lamp unto his/her feet and a light to guide their pathway.
AMEN
Please cancel every trick and every plan of the enemy concerning my children.

Daughter(s):

_____

Son(s):

_____

Family Member(s) & Friends:

_____

_____

_____

_____

Answered Prayer

*L*ord, I thank You for hearing and answering my prayer in Jesus' Mighty and Holy Name. I want to shower You with praise for the excellent things You have done for my family. I love You, Jesus and thank You for Your loving kindness and tender mercies toward me. I thank You for the knowledge that Your blessings are fresh and new every day. AMEN

Prayer to Mend Brokenness

Often, I am lost for the right words to say to my child(ren) that can bring comfort in times of frus-trations, disappointments, and loss. I ask you, sweet Holy Spirit, to inspire me with words of en-couragement that will mend my child(ren)'s heart(s) and heal the wounds of life.

Words of Encouragement to Your Children

_____

_____

_____

_____

_____

_____

_____

_____

_____

_____

_____

Prayer For Families Dealing With Death

Prayer for Strength

Lord, I am torn with emotions and feelings of total confusion and loss. I know You are my strong tower. I ask You now to give me the strength to run to You.

Please hide me beneath Your feathery wings and give me strength to endure. I need Your hope. Yet, my soul is satisfied that You are with me.

I thank You for being my friend. I honor that Your grace is sufficient for me. I am rescued by the love that I feel flowing from Your heart to mine. Please regulate my thoughts and be the compass to navigate me in this time of separation from those I love. I will rejoice in the love that was shared.

I will honor the time, talents, laughter, and love that kept us. I surrender my thoughts, tears, and sadness into Your hands. I am Yours and You are mine. This day I turn every thought, situation, and pain to You.

Lord, let me rest in you. Thank You for being my friend and an ever-present help in times of trou-ble. AMEN

I Am An Overcomer Prayer

Lord, I have battled with doubt and fear for most of my life. I have accused others in my mind and outwardly; I have used the blame game against everyone except myself. I have battled the demons of uncertainty and fought to maintain a sense of wholeness.

I kept searching outwardly for truth that was always inside of me. I was told to become free from my yesterday, I had to love me just as I am. Flaws are not indicators of weakness but sources of power that leads to transformation.

I was counseled to pray for wisdom and seek above all things, understanding. I was advised to write down my accomplishments and value those more than the disappointments. I was pushed to believe in myself and in the power inside of me called the Holy Spirit.

I learned that nothing will ever change in my life until I recognize that I deserve more. I am enough. I am strong enough and wise enough to love me. I press forward daily realizing my past is behind me. I must press forward with hope, faith and love.

Today, I love me. I am daily growing, changing and becoming new. I receive forgiveness and give it back to the universe. I accept that I am a new creature in Christ. I press toward the higher calling in Christ Jesus.

Thank You for making me an overcomer. AMEN

Casting Out Demons

Dear God,

I ask You in the Name of Jesus to cancel every trick and every plan of the enemy sent, seen and unknown to man.

I thank You now for hearing and answering my prayer. I now declare and decree that by the stripes of Your Son Jesus, I am healed.

No weapon formed against me or my seed or the seed of my seed shall prosper. I decree that I am healthy, wealthy and wise.

I thank You now that every evil spirit, every dart sent by the enemy, has been uprooted and de-stroyed.

I am covered by the Blood of Jesus and loosed and set free by the grace that rest on my life. My Soul is satisfied in You. I am healed, delivered and set free in Jesus' Name. AMEN

Prayer for Broken Marriages

Heavenly Father,

I come to You knowing it is in You that I live, move and have my being. Lord, please restore my broken marriage, as Your name is *Elyashib*, "God Restores."

I look to You because You created marriage. You alone can define marriage and put two people together. I believe Your Word, and I receive total restoration in marriage. It is in the Matchless Name of Jesus I pray, AMEN

1 Kings 17:17-24

JOEL 2:25-26

Prayer for Mothers Separated from Their Children

Sovereign God,

You know everything, and You see everything. Lord, nothing can ever take You by surprise. I thank You because You promised me at the appointed time I will be brought back into contact and total relationship with my children.

You told us, children were a heritage from the Lord, and the fruit of my womb is blessed. Therefore, I believe I receive Your Word; it is established, and it cannot be otherwise regarding my children.

Thank You in advance for Your wondrous miracles. AMEN

MATTHEW 19:14

PROVERBS 22:6

PROVERBS 17:6

1 John 3:1

Prayer to Heal Sick Children

Dear God,

I love You. I know that I am a chosen steward over the child(ren) You have blessed me with. I thank You now that by Your stripes my child(ren) is/ are healed. Your name is Jehovah Rapha and You are HEALER.

I thank You that the effectual fervent prayer of a righteous man avails much, and so I thank You for answering my prayers. The desires of the righteous will be granted and thank You now, in faith, for Your wondrous works and mighty deeds to the children of men.

All praises be to You for everything You have done. Amen and Praise God. AMEN

JEREMIAH 33:3

Psalm 103:3

Psalm 50:15

Prayer for Caretakers/Providers

Dear Lord,

Please bless those who are selfless and who give so much of themselves for the wellbeing of oth-ers. As they provide care for their fellow sisters and brothers in You, provide them with blessings, increase and favor for all they do.

Lord, bless the works of their hands and allow everything they do to prosper as You promised. We ask these blessings and many others over them in Jesus' Mighty Name, AMEN

PROVERBS 19:17

MATTHEW 25:40

Prayers Against Offense and Conflict

Teach me patience to listen, to hear, to love and to ignore the sometime painful words that flow from my loved one's mouth. I need help with not taking offense. My heart aches at seeing the pain, stress and loss that screams through their wandering eyes.

I see in my Mom/Dad, Brother/Sister, Daughter/Son such uncertainty and sadness.

Your Word says to take no offense. I desperately pray today that You would teach me to not take offense at what often seems cruel and intentionally mean actions. I recognize that it is their pain lashing out. I know that they love, value, and appreciate me.

Help me to laugh like I heard the same conversations for the first time. Teach me to remember to always wear a smile and speak only words of encouragement.

Daily remind me that the love of God in me will see me through with joy and peace.

Let my heart always be filled with love and my mind determined to bring joy to each day of their lives.

Psalm 46:1

Psalm 54:4

Hebrews 13:6

HEBREWS 13:6

Help Me Love Myself

By: Dr. Mary Coleman

Dear God,

Help me love myself more. Teach me how to pray. I seek Your grace and mercy. I am crawling back to a place of grace, away from shame and loathing, into the nautical twilight of a brand-new day.

A Prayer for Land and Sea

By: Dr. Mary Coleman

Dear God,

Teach me, to protect the beauty of the land, sea and air. Show me how-to live-in peace and harmo-ny with the environment. Give us, each one, a thoughtful heart and a wise mind.

Thank You for making humankind the guardians of nature, in care of its sustain-ability. Light our pathways as we hand to the next generation the care and feeding of our planet, In Jesus' Name. Amen.

Prayer for Children Having Diffi-culty Passing Test

Lord, my child is anxious and very fearful of failing school. Please help my child pass his/her State Exams, ACT's, and Praxis exams to matriculate to the next grade or graduation.

I need You, Father, to help me help my child to know their value. You said I could ask You for anything and if I have faith to believe that it would come to past. I believe that all things are possi-ble to those who believe.

I believe You will help my child pass this exam. This is my prayer dear God. I ask You to send the Angels of Mathematics, Social Studies, Reading and Language Arts to guide the hands of my child while testing.

Please increase my child's confidence in their ability to take and master test. Increase their wisdom, knowledge and understanding even now. I thank You in advance that my child has passed the test and is now on the way to their next class or graduation. AMEN

I was born for purpose. Raised for success. Washed from the fear of failure. I am transformed and blessed. I will push, press and win.

Dr. Carolyn Coleman

Prayers For Victims Of Abuse

Be healed from every adversary

Affirmation: I am now healed from every adversity in my life.

Be delivered from every shame

Affirmation: I am now healed from every childhood and adulthood shame. I am free to love me!

Be set free from every doubt

Affirmation: I am set free now from doubt and fear. I am confident in my ability to make sound decisions.

Be baptized from every failure

Affirmation: I am a success. I am Successful. I am resurrected from me. Every failure in my life opened a door to success.

Be rescued from every pain that made you want to quit and give up

Affirmation: I am delivered from the pain of lack. I am not a quitter. I am a Winner!

Be Resurrected from the belief that
you are not good enough

Affirmation: I am enough in every way. Every obstacle was a doorway to greatness and a window of opportunity.

_____

Affirmation: Write your own.

_____

Affirmation: Write your own.

_____

Affirmation: Write your own.

_____

Affirmation: Write your own.

_____

Affirmation: Write your own.

BE HEALED NOW IN JESUS' NAME!

Prayer for Veterans

Lord, help us honor our Veterans. Bless them to know that their sacrifice for this country and na-tion is recognized. We may never be able to identify or understand their pain. But may our love heal some of the hurt and feel the fault of uncertainty in their mind, heart and soul.

To all Veterans: know that you are loved. You are not hidden but a visual hero worthy of admira-tion and respect. We pray for your mothers and fathers, sisters and brothers, and your wives and children.

We extend our hearts and hands to each of you. Thank you for your service and your sacrifice.

I pray peace, love, joy, prosperity, hope and ultimate victory in your life.

Now Lord, fill Your soldiers with peace that will surpass man's understanding.

AMEN

List any names of Veterans you know:

Dream Big Prayer

Lord, You said that I have not because I have asked not. Today, I come boldly before you to seek your vision and provision to make my dreams a reality.

I desire to build schools to educate babies in the womb. I pray and petition to own and operate mul-timillion-dollar corporations for youth development, inventions, and new technology to cure infec-tions and diseases.

Bless me to open Think Tanks, and Entrepreneurial Centers for school-aged children.

I go in agreement with Your word that You will help me obtain wealth. Wealth to build safe senior living facilities for our parents and grandparents.

Help me to develop an "At Home Comfort Care Program" for seniors who want to live at home. So that seniors who have loss husband, wives and children do not have to lose or leave their home feeling broken and abandoned.

I ask You to bless my books, songs, poems and plays to educate, entertain, and change lives. In-crease and multiply my income, knowledge, and sphere of influence around the world in thousand-fold and beyond.

I thank You for hearing and answering my prayer in Jesus Name.

Amen (Let It Be So)

Let My Child Be

Jask You, Father God, in the Name of Jesus that You would bestow these blessings upon my child(ren).

Let My Child

- Be healed from negative thoughts and daily adversities

- Be delivered from every shame

- Be set free from every doubt

- Be helpful and considerate daily

- Be baptized from every failure

- Be rescued from evil thoughts and evil people

- Be honest with self and true to what is right

- Be protective of the universe

- Be a great servant leader

- Be a wealth maker

- Be a world changer

- Be a light in darkness

- Be bold and very, very courageous

You Are Old Enough To...

I ask You to help my child to stand when life shoots its arrow of defeat. Please give them strength and courage to stand strong, fight the good fight and win.

- ❧ You Are Old Enough To:

- ❧ Fall and get back up again and win

- ❧ Forgive and be healed from life disappointments

- ❧ Admit when you are wrong

- ❧ Know the importance of saying I am sorry and meaning it

- ❧ Know you don't have all the answers

- ❧ Laugh at yourself but never at others

- ❧ That your feelings matter

- ❧ Know that you are enough

- ❧ Know life is what you make it

- ❧ Know love is worth fighting for

- ❧ Know you are a precious gift from God

My Personal Affirmations

Write your own affirmations. Put them somewhere visible and review them daily. Trust in the power within yourself to change your own situation, by faith.

Time of reflections and growth evaluation

What Have I Learned?

How Has My Prayer Life Changed

(post images?)

What is next in my life chart

What Provision Do I Need From God?

What Relationships Need To Be Mended?

What Relationships Are Toxic And Must End?

What Habits Must I Change?

What buried emotions are keeping me from moving forward and living your best life possible? Do I need to seek counsel-ing?

What are my goals for the next three (3) months?

What are my Spiritual Goals?

How much time will you commit to prayer daily?

How often will you read the Bible each day?

How much time will you spend in prayer?

What assignments will you do for God?

What financial goals are you setting for yourself right now?

How will you invest, save, and accomplish this?

About the Author

Dr. Carolyn Coleman

Dr. C.C. "The Lady of Wisdom"

BISHOP CAROLYN COLEMAN is affectionately known as "Dr. CC", The Lady of Wisdom. Her ministerial credentials, pastoral record, teaching career, honors and awards, publications, board memberships, appointments, list of distinguished collaborators, academic synergistic activities, and creative talents are extraordinary. She is Founder and Bishop of Tabernacle of Alpha & Omega Non-Denominational Church in Jackson, Mississippi.

She received a Bachelor of Science in Mass Communications with emphasis on Radio, Television and Public Relations, and a Master of Science in Library Science and Educational Technology from Jackson State University (JSU), and the PhD in Philosophy and Human Relations from The Dayspring Christian University. She is also a Certified Licensed Christian Master Life Coach (from the American Association of Christian Therapists Inc.).

Dr. Coleman is the Executive Director of Tabernacle Community Outreach Mentoring Program, and the Founder and Executive Director of C Square Educational Resource Center "An Accredited Academic Institution" in Jackson, Mississippi.

She has served as Executive Director of Kids Kollege at Jackson State University and the Executive Director of Children Defense Fund Freedom School, also at JSU.

In 2017, Bishop Coleman was appointed Academic Dean of DCCJ Kingdom Theological Seminary. Among her many honors is the President's Higher Education Community Service Award for Excellence in Hurricane Relief Service.

About the
Contributing Author

Dr. Catherine Coleman-Smith has a EdD in Education and has received numerous awards in the field of Education. She is an entrepreneur, mentor and advocate for children and adults. She is the Founder of Crowned In Royalty Academy. Her works include: *What It Takes To Rebuild A Village After Disaster: Stories From Internally Displaced Children and Families of Hurricane Katrina and Their Lessons to Our Nation.*

Dr. Catherine Coleman-Smith is the hub of versatility and strength for this generation.

Acknowledgments

To my daughter, Catherine Nichole Coleman-Smith. You have been my wind, my push, and my press. Thank you for your heart of love, devotion, and commitment to loving God. Thank you for your inspiration and help in writing this book of prayers. Your faith in my prayers and in the power of God's Word is like a fresh breeze on a hot, sunny, summer's day.

You spent a decade of your adult life working with me. Often your genius and creativity were cred-ited to me instead of you. I always validated you, but you could have become bitter and resentful toward me. Instead you pushed me as much as I pushed you. It did not make you bitter or resentful it made you want more for me as I did for you.

Often your work was contributed as my work. I fully recognize your gifts and talents and thank God for you. Fly high my daughter knowing when others overlook you God will acknowledge and promote you.

I deeply appreciate your help on this book as well as the many books, projects, grants, courses, and adventures we shared. I am your mother, but time has made you a brilliant colleague and friend.

I want to thank you mama, Catherine Coleman-Myers, for making me believe that I could do and be anything I wanted to be in life. Your love of God was my compass. You taught me how to pray and conquer fear through the gift of prayer.

To my granddaughter Amiel Smith. I charge you to Dream Big, Go Big and Win Big in Life. The God in you will teach and empower you as you seek Him in prayer. You are the gift that causes me to rise and dares to become more. You inspire me, love Nana.

To my wonderful sisters, Linda Coleman and Mary Coleman, thanks for being my big sisters. Your lives have influenced my prayer life and elevated my understanding of love, family, and friends. Thanks for being my friend and sister.

To my nephew, Kiese Laymon. I love you and thank you for your beautiful heart and loving spirit. You are the epitome of hope, faith, love and forgiveness wrapped in flesh. I love you and daily call your name in prayer.

Join The Lady Of Wisdom
Women Of Wisdom
Membership Subscription

www.drcctheladyofwisdom.com

MEMBERSHIP REWARD PROMOTION

Each Quarter you will receive a special
Anointed Oil from Dr. CC's Collection.

WOW Membership Subscription Package Includes:

- Nine (6) Master Class Per Year

- Two (2) 30-minute Coaching Session (4) four times per year or Four (4) Fifty-Minute Counseling Sessions (1 each quarter)

- Three 911 Emergency calls per year

- Private Facebook Meetings

Membership Fee is $49.99 per Month

For more information on
Women of Wisdom Membership
Subscription visit: www.doctorcclifecoach.com

For information on the Christian Education Division of
CSquared Education visit:
www.csquarededucation.com

Dedication

I dedicate this book to my Mama, Catherine.

You have been and are the most influential prayer warrior and best friend that anyone could have in life. I dedicate this book to you with a grateful heart of thanks for all the prayers and encouragement you have given me and countless others. I would have never been able to defeat my demons and pray for others to conquer theirs without your prayers. Thank you.

I thank you for making me believe that I could do and be anything I wanted to be in life. Your love of God was my compass. You taught me how to pray and the power of prayer. The night I heard you calling my name in prayer awakened and revealed my divine purpose. I had instantly fallen in love with the power that comes through prayer.

I knew that the God in me was alive and actively seeking me out for a divine, yet unknown purpose. Today, I realize that purpose was to help others, through the power of prayer, to gain victory over the enemy from within and without.

I promise that I will continue to pray without ceasing and help others learn the power of prayer. I will teach others how to war and win with prayer. I will push forward your words to me:

> *"Don't stop praying about it until God fixes it. While you are waiting in faith for the answer, tell God 'thank You'. Why? Because it's already done. Every answer you are seeking you will find inside of you. For the God in you will keep you and bring all things to your remembrance. Ask in faith, trust God, fear not and act when you hear him calling your name.*

On rainy and cold days in my life I hear you saying, "God is good all of the time. On your worst day God is still good. I know He is good because He's been good to me".

Yes, God is good, Mama. Thank you for every life lesson that you have taught, shared and exhibited in your life. I would not have been able to conquer the storms and overtake the mountains of pain and doubt that comes with life without your inspiration, courage, fierceness and faith to always come out the winner on the other side.

As a young teen I saw you deal with the wounds of betrayal. Yet, you held your head up high. You walk in a grace that could only be given by God. You refused to bow to despair and become bitter.

Instead, you walked in a peace that spoke to me unknowingly that said you are strong, faithful and determine to overcome every storm.

You taught me that it is up to me to chart my destiny and define my success. You said happiness, peace, love, joy, determination and abundance is a choice. That no one-person should ever be seen or deemed as rejection. It is just one-person opinion. Next.

At 91-years-old, Mama, you still inspire and encourage me. I still hear you calling my name in prayer. It still brings me joy and causes my heart to skip a beat and shout 'thank You God for Mama' for all the love and inspiration you have given to your children, grandchildren, great grandchildren, numerous community children and adults. Kudos to you!

I am not afraid to walk alone. Nor am I afraid to ask for help. Nor am I afraid to boldly challenge myself and others to pray in faith, and know that it's already done!

Thank you, Mama.

www.ingramcontent.com/pod-product-compliance
Lightning Source LLC
Chambersburg PA
CBHW062009150426

42812CB00013BA/2585